[LEAVINGS]

Other Books of Poetry by Wendell Berry

WENDELL BERRY
LEAVINGS

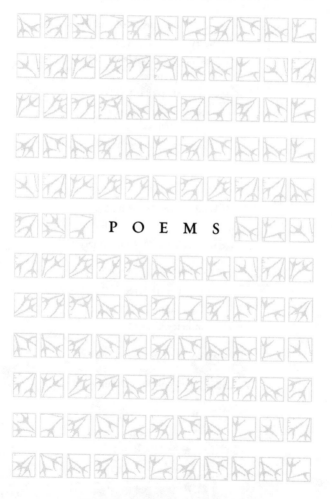

POEMS

COUNTERPOINT

BERKELEY

Please note that the ends of the following pages
indicate a stanza break: 50, 51, 88, 92, 119.

Library of Congress Cataloging-in-Publication Data
Berry, Wendell, 1934–
Leavings : poems / Wendell Berry.
p. cm.
ISBN-13: 978-1-58243-534-3
ISBN-10: 1-58243-534-0
I. Title.
PS3552.E75L43 2009
811'.6—dc22
2009025599

Jacket design by David Bullen
Interior design by David Bullen
Printed in the United States of America

COUNTERPOINT
2117 Fourth Street
Suite D
Berkeley, CA 94710

www.counterpointpress.com

Distributed by Publishers Group West

10 9 8 7 6 5 4

I dedicate this book

with respect

to the poet John Haines

CONTENTS

Part I

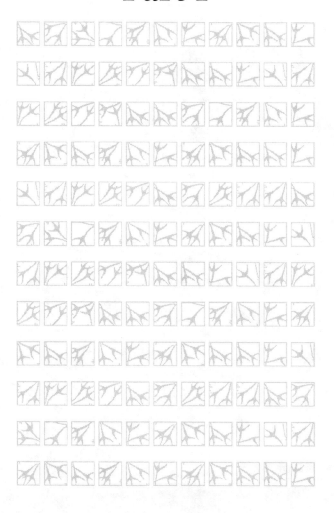

LIKE SNOW

Suppose we did our work
like the snow, quietly, quietly,
leaving nothing out.

THE SHINING ONES

While the land suffers, automobiles thrive,
shining as they glide by the dying towns,
the empty fields bare in winter,
the deserted farmhouses, obstacles merely
to an ideal trajectory from everywhere to anywhere.

ON THE THEORY OF THE BIG BANG
AS THE ORIGIN OF THE UNIVERSE

I.
What banged?

II.
Before banging
how did it get there?

III.
When it got there
where was it?

LET US HEAR FROM YOU

Over and over again
I have been thrown
to the ground.
Over and over again
I have risen up.
One of these days, thrown,
I will stay down.
Antaeus, write home!

LOOK IT OVER

I leave behind even
my walking stick. My knife
is in my pocket, but that
I have forgot. I bring
no car, no cell phone,
no computer, no camera,
no CD player, no fax, no
TV, not even a book. I go
into the woods. I sit on
a log provided at no cost.
It is the earth I've come to,
the earth itself, sadly
abused by the stupidity
only humans are capable of
but, as ever, itself. Free.
A bargain! Get it while it lasts.

A LETTER
(to Ed McClanahan)

Dear Ed,
I dreamed that you and I were sent to Hell.
The place we went to was not fiery
or cold, was not Dante's Hell or Milton's,
but was, even so, as true a Hell as any.
It was a place unalterably public
in which crowds of people were rushing
in weary frenzy this way and that,
as when classes change in a university
or at quitting time in a city street,
except that this place was wider far
than we could see, and the crowd as large
as the place. In that crowd every one
was alone. Every one was hurrying.
Nobody was sitting down. Nobody
was standing around. All were rushing
so uniformly in every direction, so
uniformly frantic, that to average them
would have stood them still. It was a place
deeply disturbed. We thought, you and I,
that we might get across and come out
on the other side, if we stayed together,
only if we stayed together. The other side
would be a clear day in a place we would know.

[8]

We joined hands and hurried along,
snatching each other through small openings
in the throng. But the place was full
of dire distractions, dire satisfactions.
We were torn apart, and I found you
breakfasting upon a huge fried egg.
I snatched you away: "Ed! Come on!"
And then, still susceptible, I met
a lady whose luster no hell could dim.
She took all my thought. But then,
in the midst of my delight, my fear
returned: "Oh! Damn it all! Where's Ed?"
I fled, searching, and found you again.
We went on together. How this ended
I do not know. I woke before it could end.
But, old friend, I want to tell you
how fine it was, what a durable
nucleus of joy it gave my fright
to force that horrid way with you, how
heavenly, let us say, in spite of Hell.

P.S.
Do you want to know why
you were distracted by an egg, and I
by a beautiful lady? That's Hell.

A LETTER

(to my brother)

Dear John,
You said, "Treat your worst enemies
as if they could become your best friends."
You were not the first to perpetrate
such an outrage, but you were right.
Try as we might, we cannot
unspring that trap. We can either
befriend our enemies or we can die
with them, in the absolute triumph
of the absolute horror constructed
by us to save us from them.
Tough, but "All right," our Mary said,
"we'll be nice to the sons of bitches."

A LETTER

(to Hayden Carruth)

Dear Hayden,
How good—how liberating!—to read
of your hatred of *Alice in Wonderland*.
I used to hear my mother reading it
to my sisters, and I hated it too,
but have always been embarrassed
to say so, believing that everybody else
loved it. But who the hell wants to go
down a rabbit hole? I like my feet best
when they're walking on top of the ground.
If I could burrow like a mole, I would,
and I would like that. I would like
to fly like a bird, if I could. Otherwise,
my stratum of choice is the surface.
I prefer skin to anatomy, green grass
to buried rocks, terra firma to the view
from anywhere higher than a tree.
"Long live superficiality!" say I,
as one foot fares waywardly graveward.

A LETTER

(to Ernest J. Gaines)

Dear Ernie,
I've known you since we were scarcely
more than boys, sitting as guests
at Wallace Stegner's table, and I have read
everything you have written since then
because I think what you have written
is beautiful and quietly, steadily
brave, in the manner of the best bravery.
I feel in a way closer to your work
than to that of anybody else of our age.
And why is that? I think it's because
we both knew the talk of old people,
old country people, in summer evenings.
Having worked hard all their lives long
and all the long day, they came out
on the gallery down in your country,
out on the porch or doorstep in mine,
where they would sit at ease in the cool
of evening, and they would talk quietly
of what they had known, of what
they knew. In their rest and quiet talk
there was peace that was almost heavenly,
peace never to be forgotten, never
again quite to be imagined, but peace
above all else that we have longed for.

GIVE IT TIME

The river is of the earth
and it is free. It is rigorously
embanked and bound,
and yet is free. "To hell
with restraint," it says.
"I have got to be going."
It will grind out its dams.
It will go over or around them.
They will become pieces.

QUESTIONNAIRE

1. How much poison are you willing
   to eat for the success of the free
   market and global trade? Please
   name your preferred poisons.

2. For the sake of goodness, how much
   evil are you willing to do?
   Fill in the following blanks
   with the names of your favorite
   evils and acts of hatred.

3. What sacrifices are you prepared
   to make for culture and civilization?
   Please list the monuments, shrines,
   and works of art you would
   most willingly destroy.

4. In the name of patriotism and
   the flag, how much of our beloved
   land are you willing to desecrate?
   List in the following spaces
   the mountains, rivers, towns, farms
   you could most readily do without.

5. State briefly the ideas, ideals, or hopes,
    the energy sources, the kinds of security,
    for which you would kill a child.
    Name, please, the children whom
    you would be willing to kill.

AN EMBARRASSMENT

"Do you want to ask
the blessing?"

"No. If you do,
go ahead."

He went ahead:
his prayer dressed up

in Sunday clothes
rose a few feet

and dropped with a soft
thump.

If a lonely soul
did ever cry out

in company its true
outcry to God,

it would be as though
at a sedate party

a man suddenly
removed his clothes

and took his wife
passionately into his arms.

AND I BEG YOUR PARDON

The first mosquito:
come here, and I will kill thee,
holy though thou art.

DAVID JONES

As the soldier takes bodily form
(or dissolves) within the rubble and wreck
of war, so the holy Virgin takes
shape within the world of creatures,
and the angel, to come to her at all,
must wear a caul of birds,
his robe folded like the hills.

TU FU

As I sit here
in my little boat
tied to the shore
of the passing river
in a time of ruin,
I think of you,
old ancestor,
and wish you well.

THE DEFENDERS

I love the courage
of the little black ants
who when disturbed
come out of their old
fencepost as big dogs
come after a rat,
take hold of me,
shake me, and growl.

A SPEECH TO THE GARDEN CLUB OF AMERICA

With thanks to Wes Jackson
and in memory of Sir Albert Howard and Stan Rowe

Thank you. I'm glad to know we're friends, of course;
There are so many outcomes that are worse.
But I must add I'm sorry for getting here
By a sustained explosion through the air,
Burning the world in fact to rise much higher
Than we should go. The world may end in fire
As prophesied—*our* world! We speak of it
As "fuel" while we burn it in our fit
Of temporary progress, digging up
An antique dark-held luster to corrupt
The present light with smokes and smudges, poison
To outlast time and shatter comprehension.
Burning the world to live in it is wrong,
As wrong as to make war to get along
And be at peace, to falsify the land
By sciences of greed, or by demand
For food that's fast or cheap to falsify
The body's health and pleasure—don't ask why.
But why not play it cool? Why not survive
By Nature's laws that still keep us alive?
Let us enlighten, then, our earthly burdens
By going back to school, this time in gardens
That burn no hotter than the summer day.

By birth and growth, ripeness, death and decay,
By goods that bind us to all living things,
Life of our life, the garden lives and sings.
The Wheel of Life, delight, the fact of wonder,
Contemporary light, work, sweat, and hunger
Bring food to table, food to cellar shelves.
A creature of the surface, like ourselves,
The garden lives by the immortal Wheel
That turns in place, year after year, to heal
It whole. Unlike our economic pyre
That draws from ancient rock a fossil fire,
An anti-life of radiance and fume
That burns as power and remains as doom,
The garden delves no deeper than its roots
And lifts no higher than its leaves and fruits.

"Chance" is a poor word among
the mazes of causes and effects, the last
stand of these all-explainers who,
backed up to the first and final Why,
reply, "By chance, of course!" As if
that tied up ignorance with a ribbon.
In the beginning something by chance
existed that would bang and by chance
it banged, obedient to the by-chance
previously existing laws of existence
and banging, from which the rest proceeds
by the logic of cause and effect also
previously existing by chance? Well,
when all that happened who was there?
Did the chance that made the bang then make
the Bomb, and there was no choice, no help?
Prove to me that chance did ever
make a sycamore tree, a yellow-
throated warbler nesting and singing
high up among the white limbs
and the golden leaf-light, and a man

to love the tree, the bird, the song
his life long, and by his love to save
them, so far, from all machines.
By chance? Prove it, then, and I
by chance will kiss your ass.

Jason Needly found his father, old Ab, at work
at the age of eighty in the topmost
tier of the barn. "Come down!" Jason called.
"You got no business up there at your age."
And his father descended, not by a ladder,
there being none, but by inserting his fingers
into the cracks between boards and climbing
down the wall.

        And when he was young
and some account and strong and knew
nothing of weariness, old man Milt Wright,
back in the days they called him "Steady,"
carried the rastus plow on his shoulder
up the high hill to his tobacco patch, so
when they got there his mule would be fresh,
unsweated, and ready to go.

        Early Rowanberry,
for another, bought a steel-beam breaking plow
at the store in Port William and shouldered it
before the hardly-believing watchers, and carried it
the mile and a half home, down through the woods
along Sand Ripple.

"But the tiredest my daddy
ever got," his son, Art, told me one day,
"was when he carried fifty rabbits and a big possum
in a sack on his back up onto the point yonder
and out the ridge to town to sell them at the store."

"But why," I asked, "didn't he hitch a team
to the wagon and haul them up there by the road?"

"Well," Art said, "we didn't have but two
horses in them days, and we spared them
every way we could. A many a time I've seen
my daddy or grandpa jump off the wagon or sled
and take the end of a singletree beside a horse."

To tell a girl you loved her—my God!—
that was a leap off a cliff, requiring little
sense, sweet as it was. And I have loved

many girls, women too, who by various fancies
of my mind have seemed loveable. But only
with you have I actually tried it: the long labor,

the selfishness, the self-denial, the children
and grandchildren, the garden rows planted
and gathered, the births and deaths of many years.

We boys, when we were young and romantic
and ignorant, new to the mystery and the power,
would wonder late into the night on the cliff's edge:

Was this love real? Was it true? And how
would you know? Well, it was time would tell,
if you were patient and could spare the time,

a long time, a lot of trouble, a lot of joy.
This one begins to look—would you say?—real?

Part II

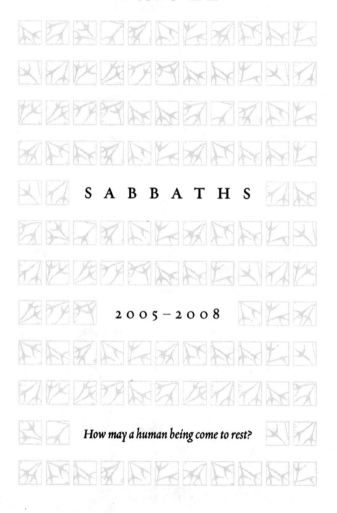

SABBATHS

2005 – 2008

How may a human being come to rest?

2005

I.

I know that I have life
only insofar as I have love.

I have no love
except it come from Thee.

Help me, please, to carry
this candle against the wind.

II.

They gather like an ancestry
in the centuries behind us:
the killed by violence, the dead
in war, the "acceptable losses"—
killed by custom in self-defense,
by way of correction, in revenge,
for love of God, for the glory
of the world, for peace; killed
for pride, lust, envy, anger,
covetousness, gluttony, sloth,
and fun. The strewn carcasses
cease to feed even the flies,
the stench passes from them,
the earth folds in the bones
like salt in a batter.

And we have learned
nothing. "Love your enemies,
bless them that curse you,
do good to them that hate you"—
it goes on regardless, reasonably:
the always uncompleted
symmetry of just reprisal,
the angry word, the boast
of superior righteousness,

hate in Christ's name,
scorn for the dead, lies
for the honor of the nation,
centuries bloodied and dismembered
for ideas, for ideals,
for the love of God!

III.

"Are you back to normal?" asks
my old friend, ill himself, after I,
who have been ill, am well. "Yes,
the gradient of normality now
being downward." For when I walk
now from rock to rock in the tumble
of Camp Branch, under the trees,
the singing stream, the stream
of light that all my life
has drawn me as it has drawn
the ever-renewing waters, I clamber
where I used to leap, where once I could
have been a ghost for all the care
I paid to flesh and bone until
some hunger turned me home.

IV.

We were standing by the road,
seven of us and a small boy.
We had just rescued a yellow swallowtail
disabled on the pavement when a car
approached too fast. I turned to make sure
of the boy, and my old border collie
Nell, too slow coming across,
was hit, broken all to pieces, and died
at once, while the car sped on.
And I cried, not thinking what
I meant, "God damn!" And I did wish
all automobiles in Hell,
where perhaps they already are.

V.

Nell's small grave, opening
at the garden's edge to receive her
out of this world's sight forever,
reopens many graves. Digging,
the old man grieves for his old dog
with all the grief he knows,
which seems again to be approaching
enough, though he knows there is more.

VI.

How simple to be dead!—the only
simplification there is, in fact, Thoreau
to the contrary notwithstanding.
Nell lay in her grave utterly still
under the falling earth, the world
all astir above, a million leaves
alive in the wind, and what do we know?

VII.

I know I am getting old and I say so,
but I don't think of myself as an old man.
I think of myself as a young man
with unforeseen debilities. Time is neither
young nor old, but simply new, always
counting, the only apocalypse. And the clouds
—no mere measure or geometry, no cubism,
can account for clouds or, satisfactorily, for bodies.
There is no science for this, or art either.
Even the old body is new—who has known it
before?—and no sooner new than gone, to be
replaced by a body yet older and again new.
The clouds are rarely absent from our sky
over this humid valley, and there is a sycamore
that I watch as, growing on the riverbank,
it forecloses the horizon, like the years
of an old man. And you, who are as old
almost as I am, I love as I loved you
young, except that, old, I am astonished
at such a possibility, and am duly grateful.

VIII.

I tremble with gratitude
for my children and their children
who take pleasure in one another.

At our dinners together, the dead
enter and pass among us
in living love and in memory.

And so the young are taught.

IX.

Here in the woods near
the road where the public lives
the birds are at their daily work,
singing, feeding, feeding
the young, as if the road
does not exist.
                    Here
by the loud road, populous
and vacant, there is quiet
where birds are singing.
                            The birds
are waiting to sing in the trees
that will grow in the quiet
that will come when the last
of the dire machines has passed,
burning the world, and the burning
has ceased.
                    And so am I.

X.

Mowing the hillside pasture—where
the flowers of Queen Anne's lace

float above the grass, the milkweeds
flare and bee balm, cut, spices

the air, the butterflies light and fly
from bloom to bloom, the hot

sun dazes the sky, the woodthrushes
sound their flutes from the deep shade

of the woods nearby—these iron teeth
chattering along the slope astound

the vole in her low run and bring down
the field sparrow's nest cunningly hung

between two stems, the young long flown.
The mower moves between the beauty

of the half-wild growth and the beauty
of growth reduced, smooth as a lawn,

revealing again the slope shaped of old
by the wearing of water and, later, the wear

of human will, hoof and share and wheel
hastening the rain's work, so that the shape

revealed is the shape of wounds healed,
covered with grass and clover and the blessèd

flowers. The mower's work too is beautiful,
granting rest and health to his mind.

He drives the long traverses of the healed
and healing slant. He sweats and gives thanks.

XI.

My young grandson rides with me
as I mow the day's first swath
of the hillside pasture,
and then he rambles the woods beyond
the field's edge, emerging
from the trees to wave, and I wave back,

remembering that I too once
played at a field's edge and waved
to an old workman who went mowing by,
waving back to me as he passed.

XII.

If we have become a people incapable
of thought, then the brute-thought
of mere power and mere greed
will think for us.

If we have become incapable
of denying ourselves anything,
then all that we have
will be taken from us.

If we have no compassion,
we will suffer alone, we will suffer
alone the destruction of ourselves.

These are merely the laws of this world
as known to Shakespeare, as known to Milton:

When we cease from human thought,
a low and effective cunning
stirs in the most inhuman minds.

XIII.

Eternity is not infinity.
It is not a long time.
It does not begin at the end of time.
It does not run parallel to time.
In its entirety it always was.
In its entirety it will always be.
It is entirely present always.

XIV.

God, how I hate the names
of the body's chemicals and anatomy,
the frore and glum department
of its parts, each alone in the scattering
of the experts of Babel.
                         The body
is a single creature, whole,
its life is one, never less than one, or more,
so is its world, and so
are two bodies in their love for one another
one. In ignorance of this
we talk ourselves to death.

XV.

The painter Harlan Hubbard said
that he was painting Heaven when
the places he painted merely were
the Campbell or the Trimble County
banks of the Ohio, or farms
and hills where he had worked or roamed:
a house's gable and roofline
rising from a fold in the hills,
trees bearing snow, two shanty boats
at dawn, immortal light upon
the flowing river in its bends.
And these were Heavenly because
he never saw them clear enough
to satisfy his love, his need
to see them all again, again.

XVI.

I am hardly an ornithologist,
nevertheless I live among the birds
and on the best days my mind
is with them, partaking of their nature
which is earthly and airy.

I live with the heavenly swallows
who fly for joy (to live, yes, but also for joy)
as they pass again and again over
the river, feeding, drinking, bathing
joyfully as they fly.

Sometimes my thoughts are up there
with the yellow-throated warbler, high
among the white branches and gray-green
foliage of the sycamores, singing
as he feeds among the lights and shadows.

A ringing in my ears from hearing
too many of the wrong things
surrounds my head some days
like a helmet, and yet I hear the birds
singing: the song sparrow by the water,
the mockingbird, whose song so beautiful
flings him into the air.

Song comes from a source unseen
as if from a stirring leaf, but I know
the note before I see the bird.
It is a Carolina wren whose good cheer
never falters all year long.

Into the heat, into the smells
of horse sweat, man sweat, wilting
foliage, stirred earth,
the song of the wood thrush flows
cool from the dark woods.

I hear the sounds of wings.
What man can abide the rule
 of "the market" when he hears,
in his waking, in his sleep,
the sound of wings?

In the night I hear the owls
trilling near and far;
it is my dream that calls,
my dream that answers.

Sometimes as I sit quiet
on my porch above the river
a warbler will present himself,
parula or yellow-throated or prothonotary,
perfect beauty in finest detail,
seeming as unaware
of me as I am aware of him.

Or, one never knows quite when,
the waxwings suddenly appear,
numerous and quiet, not there
it seems until one looks,
as though called forth, like angels,
by one's willingness for them to be.

Or it has come to be September
and the blackbirds are flocking.
They pass through the riverbank trees
in one direction erratically
like leaves in the wind.

Or it is June. The martins are nesting.
The he-bird has the fiercest
countenance I have ever seen. He drops
out of the sky as a stone falls
and then he breaks his fall and alights
light on the housetop
as though gravity were not.

Think of it! To fly
by mere gift, without the clamor
and stain of our inert metal,
in perfect trust.

It is the Sabbath of the birds
that so moves me. They belong
in their ever-returning song, in their flight,

in their faith in the upholding air,
to the Original World. They are above us
and yet of us, for those who fly
fall, like those who walk.

XVII.

Hardly escaping the limitless machines
that balk his thoughts and torment his dreams,
the old man goes to his own
small place of peace, a patch of trees
he has lived from many years,
its gifts of a few fence posts and boards,
firewood for winter, some stillness
in which to know and wait. Used
and yet whole this dear place is, whole
by its own nature and by his need.
While he lives it will be whole,
and after him, God willing, another
will follow in that membership
that craves the wholeness of the world
despite all human loss and blame.

In the lengthening shadow he has climbed
again to the ridgetop and across
to the westward slope to see the ripe
light of autumn in the turning trees,
the twilight he must go by now
that only grace can give. Thus far
he keeps the old sectarian piety:
By grace we live. But he can go
no further. Having known the grace

that for so long has kept this world,
haggard as it is, as we have made it,
we cannot rest, we must be stirring
to keep that gift dwelling among us,
eternally alive in time. This
is the great work, no other, none harder,
none nearer rest or more beautiful.

XVIII.

A hawk in flight
The clearing sky
A young man's thought
An old man's cry

XIX.

Born by our birth
Here on the earth
Our flesh to wear
Our death to bear

 2 0 0 6

I.

If there are a "chosen few"
then I am not one of them,
if an "elect," well then
I have not been elected.
I am one who is knocking
at the door. I am one whose foot
is on the bottom rung.
But I know that Heaven's
bottom rung is Heaven
though the ladder is standing
on the earth where I work
by day and at night sleep
with my head upon a stone.

II. OLD MAN JAYBER CROW

Many I loved as man and boy
Are gone beyond all that I know,
Fallen leaves under falling rain,
Except Christ raise them up again.
I know my blessings by their cost,
Thus is the pride of man made low.
To ease the sorrow of my thoughts,
Though I'm too weary now and slow,
I'd need to dance all night for joy.

III. THE BOOK OF CAMP BRANCH

Camp Branch, my native stream,
forever unreturning flows
from the town down to Cane Run
which flows to the river. It is
my native descent, my native
walk, my native thought
that stays and goes, passing
ever downward toward the sea.

Its sound is a song that flings up
light to the undersides of leaves.
Its song and light are a way
of walking, a way of thought
moved by sound and sight.

It flows as deep in its hollow
as it can go, far down as it has
worn its way. Passing down
over its plunder of rocks, it makes
an irregular music. Here
is what I want to know. Here
is what I am trying to say.

O brave Ross Feld, here is
no "fortification against time."

Here the fort has fallen
and the water passes its benediction
over the shards, singing!

How much delight I've known
in navigating down the flow
by stepping stones, by sounding
stones, by words too that are
stepping and sounding stones.

Going down stone by stone,
the song of the water changes,
changing the way I walk
which changes my thought
as I go. Stone to stone
the stream flows. Stone to stone
the walker goes. The words
stand stone still until
the flow moves them, changing
the sound—a new word—
a new place to step or stand.

In the notch of Camp Branch
the footing changes, year
to year, sometimes

day to day, as the surges
of the stream move the rocks.
Every walk, as Archie Ammons
said, "is a new walk." And so

go slow. Let the mind
step with the feet
as the stream steps
downward over the rocks,
nowhere anywhere
but where it is.

In the crease of its making
the steep stream gathers
the seeps that come silently
down from the wooded slants.
Only there at the rockbed
of the branch do the waters break
into light, into singing

of water flowing over rocks
which, in its motion, the water
moves. And so, singing, the song
changes, moved by music
harsh and crude: splashes,
slubbers, chuckles, and warbles,
the hollow tones of a bell,

a sustained pour, the small
fall steady as a column.

Sometimes, gentled, if you
stand while it flows, it seems
to meditate upon itself
and the hill's long changing
under sun and rain.

❧

A changing song,
a changing walk,
a changing thought.

A sounding stone,
a stepping stone,
a word
that is a sounding and a stepping
stone.

A language that is a stream flowing
and is a man's thoughts as he
walks and thinks beside the stream.

His thoughts will hold
if the words will hold, if each
is a stone that will bear weight,

placed by the flow
in the flow. The language too

descends through time, subserving
false economy, heedless power,
blown with the gas of salesmanship,
rattled with the sale of needless war,

worn by the mere unhearing
babble of thoughtlessness,
and must return to its own
downward flow by the flowing
water, the muttered syllables,
the measureless music, the stream
flowing and singing, the man
walking and thinking, balanced
on unsure footholds
in the flowing stream.

✦

"Make sense," I told myself,
the song of the tumbling waters
in my ears. The sense you make
may make its way along the stream,
but it will not be the stream's sense
you make, nor yet your own
quite, for the flux of language

will make its claim too
upon your walk, upon the stream.

The words fall at last
onto the page, the turning leaf
in the Book of Camp Branch
in time's stream. As the eye,
as the mind, moves from
moving water to turning page,
what is lost? What, worse,
is lost if the words falsify
the stream in your walk beside it?
To be carried or to resist
you must be a stone
in the way. You must be
a stone rolled away.

The song changes by singing
into a different song.
It sings by falling. The water
descending in its old groove
wears it new. The words descending
to the page render the possible
into the actual, by wear,
for better or worse, renew
the wearied mind. This is only

the lowly stream of Camp Branch,
but every stream is lowly.
Only low in the land does
the water flow. It goes
to seek the level that is lowest,
the silence that gathers
many songs, the darkness
made of many lights,
and then by the sun is raised
again into the air.

IV.

The times are disgusting enough,
surely, for those who long for peace
and truth. But self-disgust
also is an injury: the coming
of bodily uncertainty with age
and wear, forgetfulness of things
that ought to be remembered,
remembrance of things best forgot.
Forgive this fragmentary life.

V.

Little stream, Camp Branch, flowing
through the ever-renewing
woods on the steep slopes,
by what name did the Shawnee
call you? We live briefly in time
longer than we will live to know.
When we who know you by name
are gone, what will they call you?
When our nation has fallen as all
things fall, when the Constitution
is only another paper god, prayed to
and lied to by only another
autocrat, what will they call you?
When our kind has gone
as all things go, and you remain,
your tumbles catching and returning
light to the air as beautifully
as before, will only the angels
name you and praise you then?

VI.

O saints, if I am even eligible for this prayer,
though less than worthy of this dear desire,
and if your prayers have influence in Heaven,
let my place there be lower than your own.
I know how you longed, here where you lived
as exiles, for the presence of the essential
Being and Maker and Knower of all things.
But because of my unruliness, or some erring
virtue in me never rightly schooled,
some error clear and dear, my life
has not taught me your desire for flight:
dismattered, pure, and free. I long
instead for the Heaven of creatures, of seasons,
of day and night. Heaven enough for me
would be this world as I know it, but redeemed
of our abuse of it and one another. It would be
the Heaven of knowing again. There is no marrying
in Heaven, and I submit; even so, I would like
to know my wife again, both of us young again,
and I remembering always how I loved her
when she was old. I would like to know
my children again, all my family, all my dear ones,
to see, to hear, to hold, more carefully
than before, to study them lingeringly as one
studies old verses, committing them to heart

forever. I would like again to know my friends,
my old companions, men and women, horses
and dogs, in all the ages of our lives, here
in this place that I have watched over all my life
in all its moods and seasons, never enough.
I will be leaving how many beauties overlooked?
A painful Heaven this would be, for I would know
by it how far I have fallen short. I have not
paid enough attention, I have not been grateful
enough. And yet this pain would be the measure
of my love. In eternity's once and now, pain would
place me surely in the Heaven of my earthly love.

VII.

Before we kill another child
for righteousness' sake, to serve
some blissful killer's sacred cause,
some bloody patriot's anthem
and his flag, let us leave forever
our ancestral lands, our holy books,
our god thoughtified to the mean
of our smallest selves. Let us go
to the graveyard and lie down
forever among the speechless stones.

VIII.

We might as well require a man to wear still the coat which
fitted him when a boy as civilized society to remain ever under
the regimen of their barbarous ancestors.

Thomas Jefferson to Samuel Kercheval, July 12, 1816

How can we be so superior
to "our barbarous ancestors"?
The truth will never be complete
in any mind or time. It will never
be reduced to an explanation.
What you have is only a sack of fragments
never to be filled: old bones, fossils,
facts, scraps of writing, sprawls of junk.
You know yourself only poorly and in part,
the best and the worst maybe forgotten.
However you arrange the pieces, however
authentic, a story is what you'll have,
an artifact, for better or worse.
So go ahead. Gather your findings into
a plausible arrangement. Make a story.
Show how love and joy, beauty and goodness
shine out amongst the rubble.

IX.

"That's been an oak tree a long time,"
said Arthur Rowanberry. How long a time
we did not know. The oak meant,
as Art meant, that we were lost
in time, in which the oak and we had come
and would go. Nobody knows what
to make of this. It was as if,
there in the Sabbath morning light,
we both were buried or unborn while
the oak lived, or it would fall
while we stood. But Art, who had
the benefit of not too much education,
not too many days pressed between pages
or framed in a schoolhouse window,
is long fallen now, though he stands
in my memory still as he stood
in time, or stands in Heaven,
and a few of his memories remain
a while as memories of mine. To be
on horseback with him and free,
lost in time, found in place, early
Sunday morning, was plain delight.
We had ridden over all his farm,
along field edges, through the woods,
in search of ripe wild fruit, and found

none, for all our pains, and yet
"We didn't find what we were looking for,"
said Arthur Rowanberry, pleased,
"but haven't we seen some fine country!"

2 0 0 7

"When you get the time to do it and you drive up here
and leave your truck and walk into the woods and stay
a while in a pretty place where you don't hear no noise
and nothing's bothering you, and you go back the next
week and that place is not even there, that's hard."

Joe Begley (1919–2000) of Blackey, Kentucky,
speaking of mountain-removal coal mining

I.

I dream by night the horror
That I oppose by day.
The nation in its error
And by its work and play

Destroys its land, pollutes
Its streams, and desecrates
Air and light. From the roots
It dies upward, our rights,

Divinely given, plundered
And sold by purchased power
That dies from the head downward,
Marketed hour by hour.

That market is a grave
Where goods lie dead that ought
To live and grow and thrive,
The dear world sold and bought

To be destroyed by fire,
Forest and soil and stone.
The conscience put to hire
Rules over flesh and bone.

To take the coal to burn
They overturn the world
And all the world has worn
Of grace, of health. The gnarled,

Clenched, and forever shut
Fist of their greed makes small
The great Life. Hollowed out,
The soul like the green hill

Yields to the force of dearth.
The crack in the despot's skull
Descends into the earth,
And what was bright turns dull.

II.

The nation is a boat,
as some have said, ourselves
its passengers. How troubling
now to ride it drifting
down the flow from the old
high vision of dignity, freedom,
holy writ of habeas corpus,
and the land's abundance—down
to waste, want, fear, tyranny,
torture, caricature
of vision in a characterless time,
while the abyss whirls below.

To save yourself heartwhole
in life, in death, go back
upstream, if you have to swim
ashore and walk. Walk
upstream along the bank
of the Kentucky River, the bank
of Cane Run, and step from
stone to stone up Camp Branch
through the cut down, longtime
returning woods. Go back

through the narrowing valleys
to the waters of origin, the dry
leaves, the bare wintering trees,
the dead, the unreturning.
Go from the corrupted nation
to the ruining country. With the land
again make common cause.
In loving it, be free.
Diminished as it is,
grant it your grief and care,
whole in heart, in mind
free, though you die or live.
So late, begin again.

The abyss of no-meaning—what
can prevail against it? Love
for the water in its standing
fall through the hill's wrist
from the town down to the river.
There is no love but this,
and it extends from Heaven
to the land destroyed,
to the hurt man in his cage,
to the dead man in his grave.

Shall we do without hope? Some days
there will be none. But now
to the dry and dead woods floor
they come again, the first
flowers of the year, the assembly
of the faithful, the beautiful,
wholly given to being.
And in this long season
of machines and mechanical will
there have been small human acts
of compassion, acts of care, work
flowerlike in selfless loveliness.
Leaving hope to the dark
and to a better day,
receive these beauties freely
given, and give thanks.

III.

Yes, though hope is our duty,
let us live a while without it
to show ourselves we can.
Let us see that, without hope,
we still are well. Let hopelessness
shrink us to our proper size.
Without it we are half as large
as yesterday, and the world
is twice as large. My small
place grows immense as I walk
upon it without hope.
Our springtime rue anemones
as I walk among them, hoping
not even to live, are beautiful
as Eden, and I their kinsman
am immortal in their moment.

Out of charity let us pray
for the great ones of politics
and war, the intellectuals,
scientists, and advisors,
the golden industrialists,
the CEOs, that they too
may wake to a day without hope
that in their smallness they

may know the greatness of Earth
and Heaven by which they so far
live, that they may see
themselves in their enemies,
and from their great wants fallen
know the small immortal
joys of beasts and birds.

IV.

In our consciousness of time
we are doomed to the past.
The future we may dream of
but can know it only after
it has come and gone.
The present too we know
only as the past. When
we say, "This now is
present, the heat, the breeze,
the rippling water," it is past.
Before we knew it, before
we said "now," it was gone.

If the only time we live
is the present, and if the present
is immeasurably short (or
long), then by the measure
of the measurers we don't
exist at all, which seems
improbable, or we are
immortals, living always
in eternity, as from time to time
we hear, but rarely know.

You see the rainbow and the new-leafed
woods bright beneath, you see
the otters playing in the river
or the swallows flying, you see
a belovèd face, mortal
and alive, causing the heart
to sway in the rift between beats
where we live without counting,
where we have forgotten time
and have forgotten ourselves,
where eternity has seized us
as its own. This breaks
open the little circles
of the humanly known and believed,
of the world no longer existing,
letting us live where we are,
as in the deepest sleep also
we are entirely present,
entirely trusting, eternal.

Is it concentration of the mind,
our unresting counting
that leaves us standing
blind in our dust?
In time we are present only
by forgetting time.

V.

Those who use the world assuming
their knowledge is sufficient
destroy the world. The forest
is mangled for the sale
of a few sticks, or is bulldozed
into a stream and covered over
with the earth it once stood
upon. The stream turns foul,
killing the creatures that once
lived from it. Industrial humanity,
an alien species, lives by death.
In the clutter of facts, the destroyers
leave behind them one big story,
of the world and the world's end,
that they don't know. They know
names and little stories. But the names
of everything are not everything.
The story of everything, told,
is only a little story. They don't know
the languages of the birds
who pass northward, feeding
through the treetops early
in May, kept alive by knowledge
never to be said in words.
Hang down your head. This
is our hope: Words emerge
from silence, the silence remains.

VI.

It is hard to have hope. It is harder as you grow old,
for hope must not depend on feeling good
and there is the dream of loneliness at absolute midnight.
You also have withdrawn belief in the present reality
of the future, which surely will surprise us,
and hope is harder when it cannot come by prediction
any more than by wishing. But stop dithering.
The young ask the old to hope. What will you tell them?
Tell them at least what you say to yourself.

Because we have not made our lives to fit
our places, the forests are ruined, the fields eroded,
the streams polluted, the mountains overturned. Hope
then to belong to your place by your own knowledge
of what it is that no other place is, and by
your caring for it as you care for no other place, this
place that you belong to though it is not yours,
for it was from the beginning and will be to the end.

Belong to your place by knowledge of the others who are
your neighbors in it: the old man, sick and poor,
who comes like a heron to fish in the creek,
and the fish in the creek, and the heron who manlike
fishes for the fish in the creek, and the birds who sing
in the trees in the silence of the fisherman
and the heron, and the trees that keep the land
they stand upon as we too must keep it, or die.

This knowledge cannot be taken from you by power
or by wealth. It will stop your ears to the powerful
when they ask for your faith, and to the wealthy
when they ask for your land and your work.
Answer with knowledge of the others who are here
and of how to be here with them. By this knowledge
make the sense you need to make. By it stand
in the dignity of good sense, whatever may follow.

Speak to your fellow humans as your place
has taught you to speak, as it has spoken to you.
Speak its dialect as your old compatriots spoke it
before they had heard a radio. Speak
publicly what cannot be taught or learned in public.

Listen privately, silently to the voices that rise up
from the pages of books and from your own heart.
Be still and listen to the voices that belong
to the streambanks and the trees and the open fields.
There are songs and sayings that belong to this place,
by which it speaks for itself and no other.

Found your hope, then, on the ground under your feet.
Your hope of Heaven, let it rest on the ground
underfoot. Be lighted by the light that falls
freely upon it after the darkness of the nights
and the darkness of our ignorance and madness.
Let it be lighted also by the light that is within you,

which is the light of imagination. By it you see
the likeness of people in other places to yourself
in your place. It lights invariably the need for care
toward other people, other creatures, in other places
as you would ask them for care toward your place and you.

No place at last is better than the world. The world
is no better than its places. Its places at last
are no better than their people while their people
continue in them. When the people make
dark the light within them, the world darkens.

VII.

In time a man disappears
from his lifelong fields, from
the streams he has walked beside,
from the woods where he sat and waited.
Thinking of this, he seems to
miss himself in those places
as if always he has been there,
watching for himself to return.
But first he must disappear,
and this he foresees with hope,
with thanks. Let others come.

VIII.

Poem, do not raise your voice.
Be a whisper that says "There!"
where the stream speaks to itself
of the deep rock of the hill
it has carved its way down to
in flowing over them, "There!"
where the sun enters and the tanager
flares suddenly on the lighted branch,
"There!" where the aerial columbine
brightens on its slender stalk.
Walk, poem. Watch, and make no noise.

IX.

I go by a field where once
I cultivated a few poor crops.
It is now covered with young trees,
for the forest that belongs here
has come back and reclaimed its own.
And I think of all the effort
I have wasted and all the time,
and of how much joy I took
in that failed work and how much
it taught me. For in so failing
I learned something of my place,
something of myself, and now
I welcome back the trees.

X.

I love the passing light
upon this valley now green
in early summer as I watch
late in life. And upon the one
by whom I live, who is herself
a light, the light is passing
as she works in the garden
in the quiet. The past light
I love, but even more
the passing light. To this
love, we give our work.

XI.

The sounds of engines leave the air.
The Sunday morning silence comes
at last. At last I know the presence
of the world made without hands,
the creatures that have come to be
out of their absence. Calls
of flicker and jay fill the clear
air. Titmice and chickadees feed
among the green and the dying leaves.
Gratitude for the gifts of all the living
and the unliving, gratitude which is
the greatest gift, quietest of all,
passes to me through the trees.

XII.

Learn by little the desire for all things
which perhaps is not desire at all
but undying love which perhaps
is not love at all but gratitude
for the being of all things which
perhaps is not gratitude at all
but the maker's joy in what is made,
the joy in which we come to rest.

XIII.

"The past above, the future below
and the present pouring down . . ."
wrote Dr. Williams. Is that
correct? Or is the future above
and the past below?
                    The stream
that is departing from itself as
it was is above and is the past.
The stream that is coming to itself
as it will be is below and is
the future. Or:
                    The stream yet
to come is above and is the future.
The stream that has gone by
is below and is the past.

In its riddles in the world
in the mind in the world
the stream is the stream
beyond words, beginning nowhere,
ending nowhere.
                    It falls as rain.
It flows in all its length. It enters
finally the sea. It rises into the air.

It falls as rain. To the watcher
on the shore, it comes and it
goes.
     The immeasurable, untestable,
irrecoverable moment of its passing
is the present, always already
past before we can say that it is
present, that it was the future
flowing into the past or is
the past flowing into the future

or both at once into the present
that is ever-passing and eternal,
the instantaneous, abounding life.

2 0 0 8

I.

After the bitter nights
and the gray, cold days
comes a bright afternoon.
I go into the creek valley
and there are the horses, the black
and the white, lying in the warm
shine on a bed of dry hay.
They lie side by side,
identically posed as a painter
might imagine them:
heads up, ears and eyes
alert. They are beautiful in the light
and in the warmth happy. Such
harmonies are rare. This is
not the way the world
is. It is a possibility
nonetheless deeply seeded
within the world. It is
the way the world is sometimes.

II.

A man's desire, overwhelming
as it may seem, is no greater
than that of the male chickadee
or the yellow-throated warbler
at his high ecstatic song, no smaller
than that of the bull elephant
or whale. And so we come,
whichever way we turn, to plentitude.
The fullness of a cup equals
that of the sea—unless the mind
conceive of more, longing for women
in disregard of the limit
of singularity, gluttonous beyond
hunger, greedy for money in excess
of goods, lusting for Heaven
in excess, not only of our worth
which would be most humbling,
but of any known human power
of delectation. And so the mind
grows a big belly, a sack full
of the thought of more, and the whole
structure of enough, of life itself,
which is never more nor less
than enough, falls in pieces.
In the name of more we destroy

for coal the mountain and its forest
and so choose the insatiable flame
over the green leaf that within our care
would return to us unendingly
until the end of time.

III.

Inside its bends, the river
builds the land, outside
it frets the land away.
This is unjust only from
a limited view. Forever
it doesn't matter, is only
the world's way, the give
and take, the take and
give we suffer in order
to live. This household
of my work, ungainly on
its stilts, stands outside
the bend, and the river wears
near and near, flow
outlasting the standing firm.
Trees once here are gone,
the slope they stood upon
gone. I needed what is lost,
although I love as well
the flow that took it. Now
spring is coming, the redbird's
peal rings from the thicket,
the pair exchanges like
a kiss a seed from the feeder,
and this is timeless. But a day

in time will come when this
house will give way, the walls
lean and fall. Shattered will be
my window's rectitude.

IV.

A man is walking in a field
and everywhere at his feet
in the short grass of April
the small purple violets
are in bloom. As the man walks
the ground drops away,
the sunlight of day becomes
a sort of darkness in which
the lights of the flowers rise
up around him like
fireflies or stars in a sort
of sky through which he walks.

V.

How many of your birthdays
I have by now been
glad of! And all that time
I've been trying to tell you
how with you was born
my truest life and most
desired, the better man
by your birth I am, however
fallen short. I'll never
get it right by half.
Between us, by now, what
is more telling than the silence
in which once more an old
redbud simply blooms?

VI. THE LOCUSTS

For the third time since the first
summer we were married, they've come
again. Having stayed seventeen years
in the dark ground, they rise as if
only a night had passed, uttering
by instruction deep and great
as their long delay their ancient call:
"Pha-a-a-a-a-a-a-a-*raoh*!" as
Art Rowanberry said they say,
remembering their days as a plague
in Egypt. And yet they come young
to the light from time older than Pharaoh.
They must come young or not at all.
Our sleeps, like theirs, have carried us
through many darknesses, to wake
to plagues of our time, minds willfully
mechanical, great power ignorant
and greedy, our own complicity,
but waking to the same light the locusts
waken to, and to our work and pleasure.
Though the body grows old and bears
the ache and weight of many days,
the life by which it lives is young,
for life is young or it does not
exist, is not even dead. And so

as I walk in the land's holy Sabbath
under the tall trees, I come
at once into the old young joy
that has moved me all my life to be
here in the early morning light.
But that is a dependent joy, granted
to me thrice seventeen years
by the other joy with which I return
in evening light to you, with old
love young through many sleeps.

VII.

Having written some pages in favor of Jesus,
I receive a solemn communication crediting me
with the possession of a "theology" by which
I acquire the strange dignity of being wrong
forever or forever right. Have I gauged exactly
enough the weights of sins? Have I found
too much of the Hereafter in the Here? Or
the other way around? Have I found too much
pleasure, too much beauty and goodness, in this
our unreturning world? O Lord, please forgive
any smidgen of such distinctions I may
have still in my mind. I meant to leave them
all behind a long time ago. If I'm a theologian
I am one to the extent I have learned to duck
when the small, haughty doctrines fly overhead,
dropping their loads of whitewash at random
on the faces of those who look toward Heaven.
Look down, look down, and save your soul
by honester dirt, that receives with a lordly
indifference this off-fall of the air. Christmas
night and Easter morning are this soil's only laws.
The depth and volume of the waters of baptism,
the true taxonomy of sins, the field marks
of those most surely saved, God's own only true
interpretation of the Scripture: these would be

causes of eternal amusement, could we forget
how we have hated one another, how vilified
and hurt and killed one another, bloodying
the world, by means of such questions, wrongly
asked, never to be rightly answered, but asked and
wrongly answered, hour after hour, day after day,
year after year—such is my belief—in Hell.

VIII.

Hell is timely, for Hell is the thought
that Hell will go on, on and on, without end.
Heaven is only present, instantaneous and eternal,
a mayfly, a blue dayflower, a life entirely given,
complete forever in its hour.

IX.

As if suddenly, little towns
where people once lived all
their lives in the same houses
now fill with strangers who
don't bother to speak or wave.
Life is a lonely business.
Gloss it how you will,
plaster it over with politic
bullshit as you please,
ours has been a brutal
history, punishing without
regret whatever or whomever
belonged or threatened to belong
in place, converting the land
to poverty and money any
way that was quickest. Now
after the long invasion
of alien species, including
our own, in a time of endangered
species, including our own,
we face the hard way: no choice
but to do better. After
the brief cataclysm of "cheap"
oil and coal has long
passed, along with the global
economy, the global village,

the hoards who go everywhere
and live nowhere, after
the long relearning, the long
suffering, the homecoming
that must follow, maybe
there will be a New World
of native communities again:
plants, animals, humans,
soils, stones, stories,
songs—all belonging
to such small, once known
and forgotten, officially unknown
and exploited, beautiful places
such as this, where despite
all we have done wrong
the golden light of October
falls through the turning leaves.
The leaves die and fall,
making wealth in the ground,
making in the ground the only
real material wealth.
Ignoring our paltry dream
of omniscience merely human,
the knowing old land
has lighted the woodland's edges
with the last flowers of the year,
the tiny asters once known
here as farewell-summer.

X.

So many times I've gone away
from here, where I'd rather be
than any place I know, to go
off into the air for which
my only gift is breath, for I have
of myself no wings. It is death.
Farewell, my dearest ones.
Farewell, my lovely fields. Farewell,
my grazing flock, my patient horses,
Maggie my ardent dog. Farewell,
tall woods always so full of song.

However long I've stayed away,
coming home is resurrection. The man
who has been gone comes back to his place
as he would come naked and cold
into his own clothes. And they
are here, the known beloved: family,
neighbors obliging and dear. The dead,
too, denying their graves, haunt
the places they were known in and knew,
field and barn, riverbank and woods.
The familiar animals all are here.

Coming back is brightening in a grave,
such is the presage of old hymns.
To the place we parted from in sorrow
we return in joy: the beautiful shore,
eternal morning, unclouded day.

XI.

Though he was ill and in pain,
in disobedience to the instruction he
would have received if he had asked,
the old man got up from his bed,
dressed, and went to the barn.
The bare branches of winter had emerged
through the last leaf-colors of fall,
the loveliest of all, browns and yellows
delicate and nameless in the gray light
and the sifting rain. He put feed
in the troughs for eighteen ewe lambs,
sent the dog for them, and she
brought them. They came eager
to their feed, and he who felt
their hunger was by their feeding
eased. From no place in the time
of present places, within no boundary
nameable in human thought,
they had gathered once again,
the shepherd, his sheep, and his dog
with all the known and the unknown
round about to the heavens' limit.
Was this his stubbornness or bravado?
No. Only an ordinary act
of profoundest intimacy in a day

that might have been better. Still
the world persisted in its beauty,
he in his gratitude, and for this
he had most earnestly prayed.

XII.

My people are destroyed for lack of knowledge . . .

Hosea 4:6

We forget the land we stand on
and live from. We set ourselves
free in an economy founded
on nothing, on greed verified
by fantasy, on which we entirely
depend. We depend on fire
that consumes the world without
lighting it. To this dark blaze
driving the inert metal
of our most high desire
we offer our land as fuel,
thus offering ourselves at last
to be burned. This is our riddle
to which the answer is a life
that none of us has lived.

XIII.

                              William Safire, 1986

By its own logic, greed
finally destroys itself,
as Lear's wicked daughters
learned to their horror, as
we are learning to our own.
What greed builds is built
by destruction of the materials
and lives of which it is built.
Only mourners survive.
This is the "creative destruction"
of which learnèd economists
speak in praise. But what is made
by destruction comes down at last
to a stable floor, a bed
of straw, and for those with sight
light in darkness.

ACKNOWLEDGMENTS

Wendell Berry and Counterpoint are grateful to the
following people and magazines for previous hospitality
to many of these poems:

"A Letter (to my brother)," "A Letter (to Hayden Carruth),"
    "An Embarrassment," "David Jones," "Tu Fu" first
    appeared in *Cutthroat*
"And I Beg Your Pardon" first appeared in *Wilderness*
"A Speech to the Garden Club of America" first appeared in
    The New Yorker
"Like Snow" first appeared in the *Gnomon Press 40th Anniversary
    Portfolio*
"On the Theory of the Big Bang . . . " (I), "Let Us Hear from
    You," "Look It Over," "A Letter (to Ed McClanahan),"
    "Give It Time" first appeared in *Appalachian Heritage*
Poems IV ("The times are disgusting enough") and VIII
    ("Before we kill another child") from "Sabbaths 2006"
    first appeared in *Waxwing* (Ireland)
"Questionnaire" first appeared in *The Progressive*
"Sabbaths 2005" first appeared in *Shenandoah* and in the
    Temenos Academy Review (England)
"Sabbaths 2006" was published as a chapbook by Larkspur
    Press in Monterey, Kentucky. It was also published in
    Christianity and Literature.
"Sabbaths 2007" first appeared in *The American Poetry Review*
"The Defenders" first appeared in *Orion*
"While Attending the Annual Convocation" first appeared
    in *Harper's*

INDEX OF TITLES AND FIRST LINES
(Titles are in italics, first lines in roman.)